LIFEWAYS

The Cree

RAYMOND BIAL

Marshall Cavendish
Benchmark
New York

SERIES CONSULTANT: JOHN BIERHORST

ACKNOWLEDGMENTS

A number of individuals and organizations helped in the photography, research, and writing for *The Cree*. I would like to acknowledge the wonderful people in Chisasibi near James Bay in northern Quebec. I would especially like to thank Sam Cox, who kindly guided me through the ancestral homeland of his people. My days with Sam were among the very best of my life.

I am again very thankful to my editor Christina Gardeski for overseeing this book through editing to production and John Bierhorst for his thoughtful review of the manuscript. As always, I would like to express my deepest appreciation to my wife, Linda, and my children Anna, Sarah, and Luke, who have long provided such a wellspring of inspiration.

Marshall Cavendish Benchmark
Marshall Cavendish
99 White Plains Road
Tarrytown, New York 10591-9001
www.marshallcavendish.us
Text copyright © 2006 by Raymond Bial
Map copyright © 2006 by Marshall Cavendish Corporation
Map by Rodica Prato

Library of Congress Cataloging-in-Publication Data

Bial, Raymond
The Cree / by Raymond Bial.
p. cm. — (Lifeways)
Includes bibliographical references and index.
ISBN 0-7614-1902-0
1. Cree Indians—History—Juvenile literature. 2. Cree Indians—Social life and customs—Juvenile literature. I. Title. II. Series: Bial, Raymond. Lifeways

E99.C88B55 2005
971.2004'97323—dc22
2004022394

Photo research by Anne Burns Images

Cover photos by Raymond Bial

The photographs in this book are used by permission and through the courtesy of: *Raymond Bial*: 1, 6, 7, 8–9, 11, 20, 31, 32, 34, 36–37, 39, 41, 44, 46, 51, 53, 57, 58, 60–61, 67, 69, 90–91, 93, 94, 96, 98, 100-101. *Hudson's Bay Company Archives*: 15, 65, Archives of Manitoba 1987/363 I-67/2. *McCord Museum*: 22–23, 25, 54, 72–73, 81. *Royal Ontario Museum*: 28. *Corbis*: 75, 83, 111 Bettman. *Archives and Library of Canada*: 77. *Saskatchewan Archives*: 85, 105, 107, 108, 109, 110, 112.

Printed in China
6 5 4 3 2 1

This book is respectfully dedicated to the Cree who have lived for thousands of years in the sprawling forests, muskeg, and northern plains of Canada.

Contents

For countless generations, many Cree have lived in the far north in what is now the Canadian province of Quebec.

Author's Note

AT THE DAWN OF THE TWENTIETH CENTURY, Native Americans were thought to be a vanishing race. However, despite four hundred years of warfare, deprivation, and disease, American Indians have not gone away. Countless thousands have lost their lives, but over the course of the twentieth century the populations of native tribes grew tremendously. Even as American Indians struggle to adapt to modern Western life, they have also kept the flame of their traditions alive—the language, religion, stories, and the everyday ways of life. An exhilarating renaissance in Native American culture is now sweeping the nation from coast to coast.

The Lifeways books depict the social and cultural life of the major nations, from the early history of native peoples in North America to their present-day struggles for survival and dignity. Historical and contemporary photographs of traditional subjects, as well as period illustrations, are blended throughout each book so that readers may gain a sense of family life in a tipi, a hogan, or a longhouse.

No single book can comprehensively portray the intricate and varied lifeways of an entire tribe, or nation. I only hope that young people will come away with a deeper appreciation for the rich tapestry of Indian culture—both then and now—and a keen desire to learn more about these first Americans.

1. Origins

To this day, many Cree make their home not far from the rocky shores of James Bay.

FOR THOUSANDS OF YEARS, THE CREE HAVE INHABITED A VAST TERRITORY IN what is now Canada. Having no written language, the Cree relied on stories to keep their history and traditions alive from one generation to the next. Through the long winters, people gathered around the fire in their warm lodges and listened to these stories, which recounted their beliefs, history, and customs. Here is one such story about the origin of the Cree:

The Creation

At one time, long ago, the earth was covered with water. Floating upon the surface of the water, the animals longed for dry land. The muskrat offered to dive down and try to bring up some mud. He plunged deep into the water but barely reached the bottom. He returned to the surface, gasping for air. On his skinny tail, he carried a little mud, but it was not enough. The bit of mud immediately sank back to the bottom. Then the otter dove down to the bottom, but he too failed to bring back enough mud on his slender tail. Finally, the beaver tried. He was gone for a very long time. All the other animals thought that he surely must have drowned. However, at last the beaver popped to the surface. He was exhausted, but the other animals saw that there was enough mud on his broad, flat tail to form a small island. And from this island the world grew.

Early History

The ancestors of the Cree have lived in Canada for at least 6,500 years. Related by language and culture, the Cree occupied an

Along with sprawling muskeg and forests, the territory of the Cree is marked by lakes and rivers teeming with fish and other aquatic life.

enormous territory—from north-central Quebec on the east all the way to the Rocky Mountains of western Canada. With many tribes and bands, the Cree were one of North America's largest native groups. Their language was—and still is—one of the most widely spoken native languages in North America. "Cree" comes from the Ojibwe name for a member of this tribe, *Kenishteno*, translated into French as *Kristineaux* and shortened to Kris or Kri (pronounced kree). Crees refer to themselves with the term *Cree* when speaking English. But in their own language they call themselves by other terms, such as *Iyiniwak*, meaning "People," and *Nehiyawak*, meaning "Those who speak the same language."

The Cree are traditionally divided into several groups, each speaking its own variety of the Cree language. Beginning in the east are the East Main Cree, or East Cree, south and east of Hudson Bay in the Canadian province of Quebec. East Cree living along the bay are said to be "Coasters," while those who live inland are "Inlanders."

Just to the west are the West Main Cree, also called Muskegon or Swampy Cree, whose homeland is south and west of Hudson Bay. The West Main Cree have ten regional subdivisions: Abitibi, Albany, Attawapiskat, Monsoni, Moose River (or Moose Cree), Nipigon, Piscontagami, Severn, Winish, and Winnipeg.

Farther west are the Western Woods Cree, or Woodland Cree, who make their home in the northern portions of three Canadian provinces: Manitoba, Saskatchewan, and Alberta. They have three major subdivisions: Rocky Cree, Western Swampy Cree, and Strongwoods Cree.

South of the Western Woods Cree are the Plains Cree, who migrated onto the prairies of Saskatchewan in the 1700s. There they adopted many customs of the Plains tribes. The name *Saskatchewan* itself comes from a Cree word meaning "swift flowing river."

The early Cree were feared and respected as a powerful tribe living in a vast territory east of the Hudson and James bays and as far west as Alberta and the Great Slave Lake. Because of their many friendships with other native people, the Cree could freely move from one band to another and could also marry outside their tribe. By the sixteenth century, when Europeans began arriving, there were at least 20,000 Cree people. As the fur trade developed, the Cree became the hub of the largest alliance of tribes in North America.

Their traditional allies included the Assiniboine, the Blackfeet Confederacy (before 1800), and the Ojibwe, whom the Cree regarded as their cousins. Their enemies included the Blackfeet (after 1800), the Gros Ventre, Iroquois, Dakota, Inuit, and the western Athapaskan tribes.

The Cree became involved in the fur trade not long after Europeans began to explore North America. The Cree first encountered Europeans when Henry Hudson explored their territory around James Bay in 1611. He brought a knife, mirror, and some buttons that he traded for two beaver pelts. Great Britain and France, which claimed parts of Cree territory, looked for ways to acquire furs, especially beaver pelts, from Canada to satisfy the demands of fashionable Europeans. In 1670 the Hudson's Bay Company was established under British authority at the mouth of the Nelson River. This company claimed trading rights to all the land that drained into Hudson Bay. This area in Cree territory became known as Rupert's Land.

Accustomed to the rugged terrain and often extreme weather, the Cree were well suited to be trappers and traders. They made long journeys by birch-bark canoes in warm weather and by toboggan and birch-frame snowshoes in the winter. They quickly developed good relationships with the newcomers, who offered brass kettles, steel traps, rifles, blankets, cloth, and glass beads, along with metal knives, axes, scrapers, and fishhooks in exchange for animal pelts.

The British and French continued to set up trading posts in Cree country from 1690 to 1740. Intense demand for furs then prompted France to send traders westward to exchange goods with the Cree and other tribes. Beginning in the mid-eighteenth century, forts were established farther west.

Moreover, French and British trappers and traders who ventured into the wilderness of North America became very skilled in wilderness survival. They also came to appreciate native women, especially Cree women. These remarkable women could hunt game, catch fish, gather foods, prepare meals, make snowshoes, and sew clothing, including moccasins. British and French traders and trappers, known as *voyageurs*, began to live with or marry these women, which helped them form alliances with Cree bands.

Cree leaders encouraged these marriages, which assured that trade goods would be available and that there would be a steady market for their furs. The children of these marriages came to be called Métis, which is the French term for "mixed blood." The Métis

French traders and trappers often married Cree women, who ably helped them paddle the numerous rivers of the north country.

often became skilled hunters and trappers. Since they could speak both Cree and French, they also became valuable guides and interpreters in the fur trade. Over time, they developed their own culture.

The Cree had been trading with other tribes in the forests and on the plains long before the first trading forts were established in their territory. By controlling the rivers, lakes, and trails, they could help or hamper other tribes that tried to visit the trading posts. Trading became so vital to the Cree that they began to serve as "middlemen" between the Europeans and other native bands. They often played the French and British against each other— raiding the French posts in the south and the British posts in the north. They acquired firearms from the Hudson's Bay Company and completed an alliance with the Assiniboine, which allowed the Cree to expand almost to the Arctic Sea, the Rocky Mountains, and the Red River. Living near the trading posts, they swapped for European goods, which they traded to tribes living farther inland, returning with prime furs that they exchanged for more goods from the French and British. They dominated the region from the Eastmain River to the Winnipeg River and monopolized trade with the Hudson's Bay Company, which set up trading posts between 1670 and 1688 at the mouths of the Nelson, Moose, and Albany rivers.

In fact, Cree became the most commonly used language in the fur trade. Yet the Cree also became dependent on traders for cloth, blankets, tools, weapons, and other necessities. They no longer made their own tools and weapons. Cloth replaced buckskin in making clothing. People also wanted new foods, such as flour and sugar, along with tobacco and alcohol. They began to devote much of their energy to trapping and trading furs for goods of European manufacture instead of hunting, fishing, and gathering.

By the 1760s, France was losing its territory in North America. The French posts closed, and competition between British and French fur buyers ended. In 1821 the Hudson's Bay Company and another British trading company, the North West Company, merged to become the largest and most powerful fur-trading company in the world. The Hudson's Bay Company dominated nearly all the territory in Canada for many years—until 1870 when title was transferred to the Canadian government. However, while the Hudson's Bay Company prospered, the fur trade was much less beneficial to the Cree. When the beaver and other fur-bearing animals in their native territory had been trapped, and moose and caribou had been overhunted, many tribes had to move farther west. By the mid-1700s, Cree bands found a new way of life on the Great Plains. They adopted many aspects of Plains Indian culture, such as acquiring horses and hunting buffalo. Just as the horse replaced the birch-bark canoe, the buffalo replaced the beaver. It had the advantage of providing most of the Cree's needs for food, clothing, and shelter, along with many tools and household items. Having acquired horses by the mid-eighteenth century, the Plains Cree traveled great distances over the western prairies. By 1845 a Plains Cree tribe was firmly established in the West.

The People and the Land

East Main Cree people, both Coasters and Inlanders, live in an extensive lowland east of James Bay. This territory includes sweeping beaches, islands, and rivers branching through boggy land known in the north country as muskeg. The swamps are studded with wild flowers and grasses such as arrowheads, blue flag irises, and cattails. The still waters are surrounded by forests of black spruce and shrubs, such as speckled alder, labrador tea, and late low blueberry. Sedges thrive in the damp environment, and the floor of the thin forests is blanketed with mosses including feather, hair cap, and sphagnum.

This swampy land has long supported sizable populations of big game, such as caribou, moose, and black bears. Beavers, otters, lynx, and rabbits were also hunted or trapped by the Cree. Game birds, such as spruce grouse and ptarmigan, inhabited the forests, while flocks of ducks and geese flew overhead in seasonal migrations. In the coastal waters, the Cree occasionally hunted polar bears, seals, and beluga whales. They also caught many kinds of fish, including cisco, whitefish, trout, sturgeon, and pike.

During the summer, the Coasters camped along the shore and river mouths to keep away from the spongy muskeg, which bred clouds of biting insects. During the colder months, they trudged along trails in snowshoes to trading posts, while Inlanders paddled canoes along the rivers before the winter freeze.

The West Main Cree, or Swampy Cree, lived in the low-lying region west of James and Hudson bays to the Churchill River in northern Manitoba. There the muskeg was laced with many rivers

TRADITIONAL LANDS OF THE CREE

This map shows the vast territory of the Cree around Hudson Bay in the provinces of Quebec and Ontario. Later the Cree would take up residence on the western plains of Canada.

and streams, along which the Cree paddled their canoes—or easily portaged from one headwater to another. The soggy land was studded with spruce, tamarack, and willow trees, where the Cree hunted moose and caribou. Huge flocks of ducks and geese, making their annual journeys south, darkened the skies in the flyways.

The Western Woods Cree inhabited the thick forests west of Hudson and James bays, which included the northern parts of Ontario, Manitoba, Saskatchewan, and Alberta. The forest consisted of white and black spruce, along with conifers, such as tamarack, balsam fir, and jack pine. Broad-leaved trees included

The ancestral lands of the Cree are dotted with ponds, lakes, and marshes where flocks of migrating geese are a common sight.

white birch, trembling aspen, and balsam poplar. In the lowlands, a forest of black spruce and tamarack gave way to patches of tundra amid a vast number of lakes, rivers, and streams.

There, the Cree hunted elk, wood bison, and white-tailed deer, but woodland caribou and moose were their most important large game. Barren ground caribou were also hunted, if the herds happened to migrate through their territory. Black bear were especially sought for rituals. The Cree also hunted small game, such as porcupines, woodchucks, rabbits, and squirrels. They trapped a number of fur-bearing animals, including beaver, muskrat, mink, otter, lynx, marten, fox, gray wolf, and wolverine. They hunted ducks and geese and caught many kinds of fish—pike, pickerel, whitefish, and trout.

The Plains Cree originally inhabited the forests between Lake Superior and Hudson Bay. However, during the eighteenth and nineteenth centuries, bands migrated to the sweeping plains of western Saskatchewan and eastern Alberta, and south to northern Montana. Following the herds of buffalo, they lived farthest north of all the Plains tribes in North America, their range extending into the Canadian Rockies. There, they made a new home for themselves in a landscape of rolling plains and faced brutally cold winters, especially when arctic winds plunged down from the north.

Wherever they lived, the Cree adapted to the land and climate and prospered by hunting, fishing, and gathering.

2. Camps and Villages

When Cree bands moved west to the Canadian prairies, they began to hunt buffalo and live in tipis like those favored by the Plains Indians.

THE PEOPLE DRIFTED APART DURING THE FALL, WINTER, AND SPRING, BUT came together in summer camps on the lakeshores. While together, they held councils and hosted ceremonies. Among the Cree, people had to be adaptable if they were going to survive in the bush. Men hunted, went on raids, and protected their families. Women were responsible for preserving meat, tanning hides, and watching over children. Yet, to survive in the harsh environment, especially through the long winters, men and women also worked together and shared many duties.

Bands

The Cree tribes were loosely composed of several bands, each of which was made up of a number of extended families, often including grandparents and unmarried aunts and uncles. They had band leaders and territorial chiefs who were chosen for their merit and spiritual powers. However, these leaders served at the will of the people. After the Cree encountered Europeans, these leaders took charge of trade between their people and the newcomers.

Like other native people, the Cree highly valued their families. In their large family groups, aunts and uncles often acted as mothers and fathers in teaching and caring for children. Elders were loved and respected as grandmothers and grandfathers. Even distant relatives of one's own age were thought of as cousins, and those of a parent's generation were treated as aunts and uncles. People often looked after the elderly, orphans, and widows who had no family of their own. Relatives also avenged murders and other crimes against family members.

*T*he Cree gathered into bands made up of several families, including grand-parents and unmarried aunts and uncles.

In the early eighteenth century, the Plains Cree first acquired horses, which completely transformed their way of life. They relied on horses as both pack animals and mounts for travel and hunting. By the 1790s, these canoe-paddling fur trappers had become accomplished horsemen who traveled across the plains, following the herds of buffalo.

Most Plains Cree families owned several horses to carry their belongings whenever they broke camp. A few prestigious men also owned horses that had been specially trained to hunt buffalo. These buffalo horses reflected the wealth and social position of the owner. Men could trade for these valuable mounts, but most often they raided enemy camps and stole them. A horse was considered the best and most honorable gift. When a Plains Cree man died, the manes and tails of his horses were clipped as a sign of respect. If the man had been wealthy, upon his death, his many horses were given to his family and needy families in his band.

Among the Plains Cree, there were between eight and twelve loose, shifting bands named for their territory or chief. Families usually followed a chief known for his prestige and generosity. Except during war, a family could freely leave a band if they were unhappy with the chief. When a chief died, his son often succeeded him. However, although this leadership position was hereditary, an unfit heir could be rejected, and a more worthy man would be chosen. A brave and generous man could then become chief after proving himself as a hunter, warrior, and orator. Each band also had a Warrior Society, which provided leadership.

Warfare

All Plains Cree warriors achieved prestige through warfare, wealth, and generosity. Young men were encouraged to be brave fighters and skilled hunters.

The Plains Cree often raided camps, usually at night—not so much to fight an enemy, but mainly to steal as many horses as possible. Among warriors, "counting coup" was as important as killing an enemy. A warrior counted coup by riding up to an armed enemy and touching him with a lance or coup stick. This was more dangerous than shooting an enemy from a distance. A warrior who killed an enemy while under fire was more highly esteemed than a man who shot an enemy as part of an ambush.

Bravery in the face of danger mattered most, and men were ranked by their war exploits. The most courageous young fighters were honored as *Okihtchitawak*, or "Worthy Young Men." Some earned this title after their first raid. Others might have to strive for a long time before they had proved themselves. Worthy Young Men became members of the Warrior Society when they were formally asked to join the group. Individuals who distinguished themselves might someday rise to become chiefs of their bands.

The Warrior Society chose a war chief based on his proven courage and skill in battle. The war chief oversaw the dances and police functions of the Warrior Society. In times of war, he took over the general leadership of the band. Under the leadership of the war chief, the Warrior Society organized the buffalo hunts, making sure no one got too eager and stampeded the herd. The group also established the

Courageous fighters and skilled hunters, Plains Cree men joined a Warrior Society after they had proved themselves in battle.

corrals known as pounds into which buffalo were driven, supplied materials for ceremonial lodges, took care of the poor, and enforced law in the camp. Theft and other crimes were rare, and these matters were easily resolved. However, murder triggered blood revenge. If families were caught up in an ongoing dispute, the Warrior Society brought the families together in a tipi and showed them the Sacred Pipe Stem. The Plains Cree held the pipe stem in such high regard that its presence was usually enough to end the conflict. Members of the Warrior Society also guarded the line of march when the band moved camp and made sure stragglers were not left behind. Once a warrior became a member, he was not allowed to be jealous, greedy, or afraid. Each Warrior Society had its own songs, dances, and rituals.

When an important decision had to be made, a "crier" summoned the leading men to the chief's tipi. The chief then explained the matter to them. Each man spoke in order of his age and prestige within the band—the youngest first and the highest-ranking man last. This council reached a decision through consensus, meaning that everyone agreed. However, a chief sometimes listened to everyone and then make the decision himself.

Dwellings

The Cree lived in several kinds of homes: a conical summer tipi made of thick poles, hide or bark sheathing, and spruce boughs; a dome-shaped wigwam covered with birch bark, pine bark, or caribou hides; or a rectangular winter home of logs and sod. People who lived in the southern part of Cree territory usually covered their dwellings with birch bark. Farther north and west, the Cree used sheets of pine bark or animal skins from caribou, elk, or moose. Extended families of ten or more people lived in each dwelling. These dwellings had a single low doorway and a smoke hole at the top. A fire was kept burning in a pit in the center of the floor. However, the larger, rectangular lodges had two fires inside. Covered with thick layers of sod, these dwellings remained warm even on the coldest winter nights.

The Cree tipi was formed around three main poles, instead of the four or more poles used by other tribes. To make the tipi, they first cut cedar or spruce trees and peeled off the bark. About nineteen feet long, the heavy poles had to be tapered—five to eight inches at the bottom and two to four inches at the top. They tied the three longest poles together about two feet from the top and raised them, spreading out the bottom legs to form a tripod. The builders then laid about thirty poles around this frame, spacing them about one and a half to two feet apart, except for the doorway, which was about three feet wide. Two longer poles were placed on each side of the doorway, which faced east. These poles slightly extended the eastern side so the tipi was not a true triangle.

Once the poles were set up, the Cree laid fresh cedar or spruce boughs on the floor in a clockwise manner. The boughs overlapped in a circle around a fire pit left open in the center of the tipi. The green boughs provided a soft cushion and gave off a pleasant scent. The Cree then sheathed the tipi with a pie-shaped animal hide covering. They tied a cover for the door and added a twelve- to eighteen-inch-wide skirt around the bottom of the tipi, which was about

When they moved into hunting and fishing camps, the Cree set up sturdy wooden poles as a frame for their large tipis.

nineteen feet in diameter. Horizontal poles were tied across the inside of the tipi from one wall to another. These were used to hang meat and kettles over the fire pit.

In the 1700s the Plains Cree brought their woodland tipi to the western prairies and began sheathing the lodges with a covering made of buffalo hides. It is believed that the tipi style of other tribes was influenced by the Cree tipi, especially after the Plains tribes acquired horses. Horses could drag much heavier loads on sledlike carriers known as travois. Plains tipis then became much larger, often doubling

*L*arge enough to comfortably shelter ten to twelve people, Cree tipis were covered with sheets of bark or animal skins.

in length. Ten to twelve people could take shelter in a tipi. Made of twelve to twenty buffalo hides, the Plains Cree tipi was not a true cone. Its steeper rear braced the structure against the prevailing westerly winds, so that it appeared to be slightly tilted. Its doorway faced the rising sun. Its base was not a true circle, but egg-shaped with the wider end in the back.

The inside of the tipi was also lined with buffalo hides to provide better insulation. Women made the tipi, set it up, and owned it. A man had to ask permission to draw a picture of his spirit helper on the inside walls. Inside the tipi there was a fire ring, and smoke rose through an open flap at the top of the structure. On the earthen floor were beds made from bundles of dried grass or rushes over which people laid buffalo robes. Women made pillows by filling rawhide pouches with duck feathers.

Whether they made their home in the forests or on the plains, the Cree respected the living space in their tipis. In early stories, they told of a supernatural woman who traveled ahead of the hunters to set up their tipis and prepare their camp. She did such a good job that no matter where they moved, it seemed as if they were staying in the same place. Children were warned not to count the poles in their tipi or the woman's magic would be lost. Each person within a Cree dwelling also had a particular space where he or she slept—determined by age, sex, family, and marital status. The Cree followed this practice even when they lived in temporary camps. This sleeping arrangement gave each person a little privacy and a feeling that they had their own small space.

To make a sweat lodge, the Cree covered a wooden frame with hides or blankets then placed heated stones inside.

Cree camps and villages also had other structures. Band members constructed sweat lodges for purifying themselves and curing illnesses. About four feet high and six feet in diameter, these dome-shaped lodges consisted of a wooden framework over which people threw robes and blankets. Heated stones were passed through a hole in the side of the sweat lodge. Water was then poured over the hot stones, and people bathed in the rising steam. Among the Plains Cree, sweetgrass was burned and a pipe was offered in the sweat lodge. The structure was often used in the Sweat Lodge Ceremony and then abandoned. In each village, there were also menstrual lodges (where women retired for a few days each month), grounds for ceremonies, and storage pits known as caches.

Today, most Cree live in modern houses. However, many families still move out into the bush for at least part of the year—for a short hunting trip, a weeklong fishing camp, or an entire season. During the winter, they may move into a rectangular home of logs and sod called a *muhtukan*. When they move to summer camps, they might live in a tipi called a *michwaup*. These tipis are still made with cedar or spruce poles and boughs, but they are now covered with canvas instead of bark or animal skins.

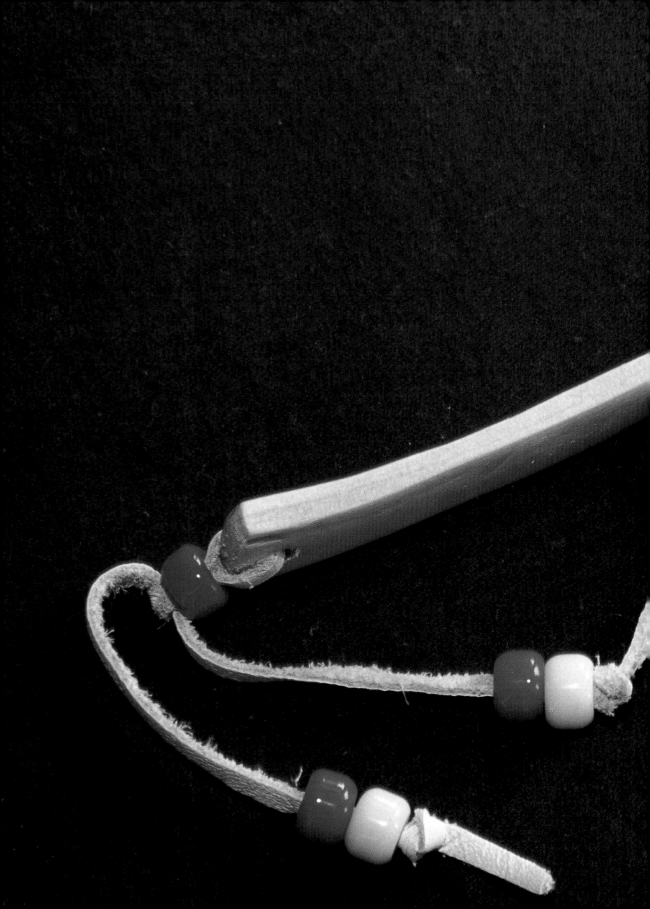

3. Lifeways

The Cree crafted many sacred objects, such as this rattle, which were used in various rituals through the course of a person's life.

Cycle of Life

The Cree were closely bound to the land and the changing seasons. Their life revolved around the daily tasks of raising children and preparing meals and the seasonal activities of gathering, fishing, hunting, and trapping. Every spring, they gathered plants in the forest. Every summer, they moved into the fishing camps. Every autumn, they trudged on snowshoes to hunt game and run trap lines. As the snows deepened around them, they settled around the fires in their lodges to listen to stories of their ancestors. Just as their lives followed the seasons, from one generation to the next, so did their customs and beliefs regarding the cycle of life from birth, childhood, and coming-of-age to marriage, old age, and death.

Birth. When a woman was about to give birth, two or three older, experienced women served as midwives. If the band was on the move, it halted briefly until the baby was born. The newborn was placed in a cradleboard, and dried moss was used as a diaper. Among the Plains Cree, the baby also wore a small pouch that held its umbilical cord, which was considered a sacred object. Within a few months, an older person named the baby after an animal, plant, the seasons, or a certain territory. There was no special naming ceremony. However, if the father had a good hunt, a feast might be held for the infant. Over the years, the child was given other names related to special events and dreams. Babies were sometimes weaned after a year, but usually nursed until they were about three

*T*his happy mother holds her child in a tipi set up for a Walking Out ceremony, a ritual that takes place at the break of dawn.

years old. When the child was about to take his or her first steps, the Cree held a Walking Out ceremony. A boy traditionally carried a small wooden gun and a girl held a wooden ax as they took their first steps outside their home in the hope that they would walk upon the earth for many years.

Childhood. The Cree cherished family life. Parents were loving and gentle to their children and taught them to respect others. They rarely punished their offspring, preferring to teach by example. During the summer, children played outside, but in the dangerously cold winters they had to be amused inside the tipi.

Parents emphasized practical training for their children. As they grew up, children helped their parents and learned the skills of hunting, fishing, and gathering. Girls were very close to their mothers and aunts from whom they learned how to take care of the household, cook meals, make clothing, and look after younger brothers and sisters. Fathers and uncles were responsible for teaching the boys. From an early age, boys became skilled with the bow and arrow in hunting and warfare, as well as building and paddling canoes, making rabbit snares, and setting beaver traps. However, since their parents were often busy providing food, clothing, and shelter, children spent a lot of time with their grandparents, with whom they were especially close.

Coming-of-Age. A feast was held for a boy when he killed his first big game. Then, as the young man approached puberty, he went on a vision quest. He traveled with his father or grandfather to a

*T*hese two girls live in the village of Chisasibi near James Bay, where their families have made their home for generations.

secluded place where they made a brush shelter. The boy was left alone to fast and pray in the shelter until he had a vision of one or more spirit helpers. These spirits presented him with gifts and rituals that would help him throughout his life. Sometimes, the boy repeated the vision quest to seek more gifts, or if he had been instructed to do so in a previous vision. Men also went on vision quests, but they rarely had visions unless they had first thoroughly purified themselves with a time of fasting.

Young women did not go on vision quests. However, when they had their first menstrual period, they had to isolate themselves in a special hut away from the band. Thereafter, whenever they had their period, they had to retire to this hut. During their first time of seclusion, young women often had visions and acquired their own spirit helpers, who might give them special powers. One of the greatest gifts that could be received in a vision was the ability to heal the ill and injured. Any man or woman who received this rare gift became a healer or shaman.

These various rituals helped to prepare young people for adulthood. After they had learned all the skills needed for survival, young women and men were ready to be married.

Marriage. Women usually married three or four years after puberty. Men usually married when they were about twenty-five and better able to support a family. When a young man fell in love with a young woman, he followed her for days without talking to her—this was his way of expressing interest in her. If she liked him, she then went home and told her parents. If her parents thought the young man would be a good match for their daughter, the father offered a gift to the young man's father. The young man and woman then sat down together in a new tipi erected by her family. She gave him a pair of moccasins, and if he accepted, the couple was considered to be married. The couple then moved into their own lodge.

Among the Plains Cree, the bride's family presented a fully equipped tipi to the couple. The father-in-law gave a horse to the groom. If the parents did not approve of the match, the couple eloped. They ran away together and settled down with another tribe. After a while, they returned to their parents, who usually accepted the couple and their marriage. Parents sometimes arranged marriages to strengthen an alliance between bands or tribes. If a couple did not get along, they separated, with either the man or the woman returning to a parent's tipi. After a while, they were free to marry again.

Death. A dying person was dressed in his finest clothing. His face was painted, and his pipe was prepared. The man then made his last requests to his family—to whom his property should be given and how his survivors should avenge his death. The Cree believed that witchcraft practiced by an enemy caused illness, so revenge had to be taken. As soon as the man died, a rifle was fired to keep the spirit of death from returning to the lodge.

The body was wrapped in bark, then either buried in a circular or oval grave, laid on a rectangular mound of earth with a wooden

The dead were reverently buried in graves or placed high on scaffolds, along with weapons, snowshoes, and a pipe.

stake fence, or placed on a scaffold. Important personal belongings, such as snowshoes, a gun and ammunition, and a pipe for smoking, were buried with the body. The drum and birch-bark canoe of the deceased were often hung in a nearby tree. After the burial, mourners expressed their anguish by grieving loudly. They then held a silent vigil for the rest of the day and night to keep the dead man's soul from returning to the family. After the funeral, the name of the deceased was never to be mentioned again. The eldest son usually succeeded his father as head of the household.

Hunting, Fishing, and Gathering

The Cree believed that the animals had been provided to them by the Creator—to give their flesh, fur, or feathers to hunters and fishermen. They further believed that plants and elements of the environment, such as the wind and water, were living spirits that could bring good weather for hunting, fishing, and gathering. The Cree also viewed themselves as part of nature, with their own complex and mysterious relationships with animals, plants, land, and weather.

The Cree hunted, fished, and gathered according to an annual cycle that followed the seasons. They trapped in the winter, hunted ducks and geese when these migratory birds were plentiful in the spring, fished in the summer, and hunted game in the fall. Armed with bows and arrows, spears, clubs, snares, and deadfalls, Cree men were renowned as great hunters of caribou, elk, moose, and beavers. They also hunted bears when they could find them and snared rabbits when large game was scarce. The Cree relied heavily on fishing as well, especially for lake trout, pike, whitefish, and pickerel. Coastal people living near James Bay sometimes speared seals and beluga whales with harpoons for meat, fat, and skins. Sealskins were made into mittens and warm boots called mukluks.

The Cree survived by traveling in small bands to hunt, fish, and gather food in the forests and along the shores of northern lakes and rivers.

The Plains Cree and a few southern groups rarely ate fish except when other foods were scarce. They caught a variety of game for meat or fur, including bears, beavers, prairie dogs, rabbits, squirrels, prairie chickens, fox, coyotes, and wolves. However, they primarily hunted buffalo, which provided most of the meat in their diet. From the buffalo they also obtained skins for clothing and tipis, hair for twisting into rope, sinew for bowstrings and sewing thread, bone slivers for needles and arrowheads, teeth for jewelry, cartilage for boiling into glue, tails for fly swatters, skulls for lamps, and buffalo chips for campfires.

Plains Cree hunters observed many customs to please the spirits and to ensure a good buffalo hunt. For example, every hunter carried his medicine pouch and hides painted with red stripes and dots. Once the scouts had located the herd, the Plains Cree hunted the buffalo in several ways. Sometimes, hunters approached downwind and then raced after the huge, shaggy animals on their horses. They galloped next to a buffalo—as close as they dared—and shot an arrow into its body from close range. Most hunters relied on bows and arrows because reloading a gun was slow and awkward on horseback. Some men also hunted with spears, which they plunged into the chests of the buffalo. Hunting in this manner called for great courage and skill.

The Plains Cree also stampeded buffalo into snowdrifts in the winter and into marshes in the summer where the huge beasts foundered and could be easily shot. They also drove buffalo into pounds. Any man who wished to build a pound had to first have a vision in which he received supernatural assurances. The making of the buffalo pound was then overseen by a shaman. The pound could only be used through one winter. The pound had a chute with a sharp corner so that the buffalo could not see the corral until they were already headed into the trap. The buffalo were steered into the chute and then shot with arrows as they milled around the corral. Before the buffalo were butchered, a shaman climbed the wall of the pound, shook rattles, and sang to the spirits.

The women, who had been following the hunt, skinned and butchered the huge beasts, then packed the meat and hides on horses and returned to camp. Buffalo meat was roasted on sticks or boiled in a pot made of the animal's stomach. Meat was also added to soups made of berries, fat, and prairie turnips. Dried and pounded meat was mixed with berries and melted fat to make pemmican, which stored well. Pemmican was essential on journeys and when game was scarce. The liver was often eaten raw; the tongue and shoulder hump were considered delicacies; and the heart was regarded as sacred.

The Cree also gathered berries and dug roots. Prairie turnip was the most important root harvested by the Plains Cree. It was eaten raw, boiled, or dried into a powder for soup. Women also gathered wild sunflower seeds, which provided an excellent protein source—either raw or roasted. They ground sunflower seeds into paste, which made a kind of butter. They also boiled the seeds, then skimmed the rich oil from the broth. This oil was used in cooking. Roasted seeds and shells could also be brewed into a hot drink. When food was scarce, the Woodland Cree boiled lichens, which were used to make a thin soup. The Plains Cree ate berries, often with dried meat, especially in August, when buffalo meat had a bad flavor. The first spring berries were not eaten until each family held its own ritual—the berries were cooked and an elder man was then asked to bless them.

Clothing and Jewelry

To make clothing for their families, Cree women carefully sewed together pieces of buckskin made from moose, caribou, deer, and elk

Here are two recipes similar to those long enjoyed by the Cree people:

Baked Lake Trout

Ingredients

One 3- to 4-pound lake trout (or other fish)
3 tablespoons sunflower seed oil
Choice of herbs to taste (dill, parsley, and/or basil)
4 tablespoons fine cornmeal

Directions

Clean and split the trout, if necessary. Place in a greased baking pan, flesh side up, and sprinkle with sunflower seed oil, herbs, and cornmeal. Bake in oven at 350 degrees for 30 minutes. Serve with pea soup, wild rice, or mixed vegetables. Serves five to seven.

Cree-Style Pea Soup

Ingredients

2 cups dried peas, soaked
16 cups water
2½ cups canned hominy
1 cup fresh celery leaves or 2 teaspoons thyme
salt
pepper

Directions

Soak peas in water until soft. Place peas in a large pot with the other ingredients, except hominy. Simmer until the peas are tender but still firm. Add the hominy and stir until soup thickens. Serves five to seven.

hides. They usually left buckskin fringes on the seams of these garments. Women also decorated clothing with beautiful quillwork, bird feathers, moose-hair embroidery, and painted designs. They preferred geometric designs and later floral patterns similar to those favored by the Ojibwe.

Men wore a breechcloth made of soft buckskin, which hung in the front and back over a narrow belt worn around the waist. They also wore hip-length leggings that were tied to the belt. Each legging was made of a piece of buckskin doubled over and sewed along the seam. Men also wore buckskin shirts. Eastern Cree people often wore tanned moosehide shirts in the summer and shirts made from warm beaver fur in the winter. The Plains Cree generally wore garments made from deer or elk hide, and occasionally buffalo hide.

Eastern Cree women wore long dresses made of two oblong pieces of buckskin sewn or laced together at the sides. Held up with shoulder straps, dresses were adorned with quillwork. The hem was often decorated with a painted design or stripes. Women usually tied a belt around their waists. Also made of buckskin, their leggings covered the lower legs and were tied just below the knee. Woodland Cree and Plains Cree women traditionally wore a wraparound skirt and a poncho-style shirt, although they later adopted the strap-and-sleeve dress. Some Plains Cree women also wore a kind of dress in which a single piece of buckskin was sewn with the seam on the side.

Both men and women wore moccasins with fringed cuffs, which were often embroidered, quilled, or beaded with beautiful designs. Moccasins had special meaning to the Cree. During a wedding ceremony,

*C*ree women often decorated garments, like this pair of moccasins, with fancy stitches, fur trim, and elaborate beadwork.

the bride offered a pair of moccasins to her future husband—so that he might walk long upon the earth. During the winter, the Plains Cree wore warm moccasins made of buffalo skin with the hair turned to the inside. The women also stuffed dried grass, prairie wool, or the longer hair from the buffalo's head into the moccasins for added protection against the cold.

Fur robes were worn by both men and women not only in cold weather but throughout the year. Cree men often wore robes made of woven strips of rabbit fur or moose or caribou hide with the hair left on for greater warmth. Some wore hooded parkas in an Inuit style. The Plains Cree wore buffalo robes with the fur turned inside. The skin side was decorated with a strip of beadwork or adorned with two rows of painted figures. Warriors occasionally decorated their garments with pictures of battle heroics. Paintings of spirits were never featured on these robes, although they were sometimes depicted on ceremonial shirts.

Both men and women wore their hair hanging loose to the shoulder. However, some women tied their hair back or over the ears. Later they began to part their hair in the middle and braid it—only the very young and the very old did not braid their hair. The Plains Cree sometimes combed their hair with the rough side of a buffalo tongue and often painted a red line along the part. The Cree wrapped the lower part of the plait with strips of hide, fur, or sinew. Warriors occasionally cut the front part of their hair into bangs, stiffened them with grease, and combed them upward.

In the winter, the Cree wore caps made of rabbit or beaver fur, with the animal's head in front and tail in back. Eastern Cree women

As cold weather approached, Cree people traditionally donned warm hats usually made of beaver or rabbit fur.

Women designed and skillfully made beautiful clothing for their families and themselves, including moccasins, mukluks, and pouches.

sometimes wore caps or peaked hoods of animal skin that were tied at the neck and often decorated with moose-hair embroidery or quillwork. Women later made these hats from wool that they adorned with beadwork and ribbons. Some Western Cree men wore peaked hats adorned with feathers. Cree men in the north also wore carved wooden goggles for protection against the glare of snow and ice. During the summer, Plains Cree men wore a sun visor made of a piece of stiff rawhide, and ceremonial headdresses such as eagle feather bonnets and buffalo horn caps. In the winter, Plains Cree men also wore fur hats that covered the face except for the eyes and nose. These were made from the fur of many kinds of animals—coyote, rabbit, beaver, and even dog. They were shaped into a band with the animal's head in front and tail hanging in the back. They often were decorated with feathers or hornlike tufts of fur. The Cree also slipped on warm fur mittens during the winter. The Plains Cree wore mittens made of rabbit fur or tanned animal skin.

Women fashioned soft leather into drawstring bags and pouches for carrying personal objects, such as sewing materials, small tools, and tobacco. Plains Cree women wove bags from buffalo hair and fibers from the nettle plant. The Cree also made leather belts, sheaths for knives, and carrying straps, which were often decorated with quillwork.

Aside from bead or shell necklaces, the Cree did not wear much jewelry. The Western Cree often pierced their noses and inserted a bead. Sometimes, the Cree also wore ornaments in pierced ears, but usually they emphasized decoration on their clothing. However, the Plains Cree did come to favor long, white, tapered tubes made from seashells, called hairpipes, as ornaments. Both men and women wore hairpipes in strings at the sides of the face or as necklaces, earrings, or pendants. Cree men also liked to wear necklaces made of grizzly bear claws strung on a folded piece of skin or fur.

The Cree often painted their faces and bodies. Men generally painted their faces, arms, and chests, while women usually painted only their chins, cheeks, and foreheads. The Plains Cree painted their faces every day. To make paints, they crushed colorful clays into a powder, mixed them with water, and baked them into small cakes. They scraped a little pigment from the cake, mixed it with grease, and painted their faces. Made from ocher, red was a favorite color. The Plains Cree painted their faces for ceremonies. Before battles, warriors daubed their bodies with white clay over which wet charcoal was laid. When they returned from the fight, the warriors painted their faces black.

The Cree also tattooed themselves by working a charcoal paste into punctures in their skin. Women tattooed the corners of their mouths while the men tattooed their entire bodies. Plains Cree men often tattooed vertical lines on their arms and chest. Plains Cree women had vertical lines on the chin.

Handicrafts

Along with making clothes, Cree women also carved useful and beautiful objects. The Cree traditionally made birch-bark cooking pots, storage boxes, and a special container for keeping hot coals. Around James Bay, they crafted woven spruce-root and soapstone

*S*killed woodworkers, the Cree shaped beautiful and useful birch-bark pots and carved wooden bowls, trays, and spoons.

kettles. Some people also shaped clay pots by coiling clay and gradually shaping and smoothing a vessel. The Cree carved wooden spoons, bowls, and trays. Other handicrafts ranged from soapstone pipes to birch-bark moose calls. Some people painted rocks with images of animals and spirits.

Men crafted wooden bows, which they fitted with bark or rawhide thongs. They made arrows and spears fitted with sharp stone, bone, or antler points. They also made crossbows of cedar wood. By the late eighteenth century, the gun had replaced these traditional weapons. Men also wove willow bark into string for making snares to catch rabbits. However, steel traps replaced both snares and deadfalls for catching fur-bearing animals.

The Cree ground stone into knives and axes and sometimes adzes. They made chisels from beaver teeth. They also honed bones into scrapers, fish spears, and fishhooks, along with sewing needles and awls. They made needle cases from the hollow bones of birds. The Cree adopted some tools from other tribes, such as a curved knife for scraping hides from the Inuit and a chisel-shaped knife from the Plains tribes. They also wove string and rope from spruce roots,

The Cree made their own snowshoes, which were essential for trudging through the deep snow as roving bands hunted game through the long winter.

willow bark, animal sinew, and animal hides. Many Cree bands wove fishnets, although other groups preferred to spear fish or catch them with a hook and line.

Among the most important handcrafted objects were those necessary to travel—snowshoes, toboggans, and canoes. Snowshoes were made in two different styles: an oval in the shape of a beavertail and a long swallowtail shape. The Cree made the frames of birch wood and the netting from *babiche*, or rawhide cord. It would have been impossible for the Cree to trudge through the deep, powdery snow without this essential footwear. The Cree made toboggans from juniper wood planks that were curved at the front end. The finished toboggan was about twelve feet long, sixteen inches wide, and just a quarter-inch thick. A leather thong was tied to the curved end and looped over a shoulder and under the arm. Women usually pulled the toboggan, but sometimes a dog was used. The Cree later adopted dog teams to pull sleds, but not until the twentieth century. The Cree made canoes with ribs of birch wood and birch-bark sheathing. They sealed the canoe with turpentine that had been boiled down until it was as thick and sticky as pitch. About eighteen inches deep and weighing eighty pounds, a birch-bark canoe could carry two adults, children, and equipment.

With these useful tools the Cree were able to travel great distances in search of food and materials for clothing and shelter.

4. Beliefs

The Cree believed in a creator,
Kitchi-Kitchi-Manito, who was present
all around them—in the air
and in the water.

THE CREE BELIEVED IN ONE CREATOR KNOWN AS KITCHI-KITCHI-MANITO, OR the Great-Great Spirit, who ruled over the world. Kitchi-Kitchi-Manito was everywhere. Lesser spirits, or Atayohkanak, often served as intermediaries between humans and Kitchi-Kitchi-Manito. Atayohkanak included a bear spirit, a deer spirit, and a spirit for every kind of tree, plant, and bird. Along with these spirits, the Cree believed in Wisahketchak, the Trickster, called Whiskey Jack in English, who could influence people's life for better—or for worse. They also feared the Matchi-Manito, or Evil Spirit, to whom they made sacrifices. This spirit brought disease, vicious animals such as snakes and cougars, and dangerous plants such as thorn bushes. Under the influence of Christianity, Matchi-Manito has gradually come to resemble the devil. Some Cree bands also recognized the existence of other powerful spirits, such as dwarfs and people-eating giants called Windigos. It was believed that these cannibals, who had hearts of ice, could possess humans and cause them to become cannibals, too. Windigos were greatly feared and anyone thought to be a Windigo was killed.

The Cree further believed that each person had a soul, called the *ahtchak*, which entered the body at birth and slipped away at death. During a vision, the ahtchak might briefly leave the body and travel with a spirit guide. After death, the ahtchak journeyed beyond the Milky Way and entered the Oskaskog-Wask, or Green Grass World. There, men, women, and children lived happy, carefree lives with no pain or hardship.

Spirits, or manitous, were thought to inhabit all other living things and phenomena, including wind and thunder. Manitous appeared in dreams and gave special protection and powers to a person. Each person had a medicine bundle, which held objects of great spiritual power. Some men and women, who received extraordinary powers from manitous, such as the ability to cure, became shamans.

Both men and women could be shamans. The Cree had several kinds of shamans, who foretold the future and cured illnesses and injuries. To heal a person, they might host a "shaking tent" ritual. Knowledge and skill with plant medicines—made from stems, leaves, roots, or the whole plant—were usually purchased or inherited from another. These medicines were used to cure everything from headaches to serious fevers. Shamans practiced rituals of singing, blowing, and sucking the disease from the sick person.

Rituals and Ceremonies

The Cree often gathered to sing, dance, and play games to mark special occasions, such as a successful hunt. They also held more formal dances, such as the Discovery Dance, in which they imitated the pursuit and defeat of an enemy before going into battle. Additionally, they held a Conjuring Dance to ensure success in war and a War Dance to celebrate their victory. The Cree enjoyed the Feasting or Greeting Dance when bands came together in the spring. To the rhythm of drums and rattles, they also had dances to celebrate animals such as the deer, caribou, and bear.

Among the Plains Cree, every band had at least one Askitci, or pipe stem bundle. The Cree believed the Great Spirit gave the pipe stem bundle to the first human being to help keep the peace. The bundle held the Sacred Pipe Stem, and there could be no violence in its presence. When people quarreled, they had to make peace when the Askitci was presented to them—no matter how serious their argument. The Sacred Pipe Stem also helped to bring peace between warring tribes. The Cree used the pipe to begin all rituals and social occasions. Men passed the pipe in a clockwise direction, just as the sun moved in the sky. They made offerings and called upon the spirits, which they believed smoked with them and thus had to listen to their requests. Long strands of sweetgrass were plaited, and during ceremonies bits of the grass were broken off and burned on hot coals. The Cree believed that the fragrant smoke purified the people and their ritual.

The Sun Dance became the most important ceremony of the Plains Cree. In this sacred ceremony, young men pierced their bodies as a sacrifice to please the Creator. The Sun Dance was usually held just once a year, but another Sun Dance might be held for a special occasion. In this sacred gathering, everyone prayed and asked the spirits to heal a sick child or help with other difficulties. A Sun Dance could also be a social occasion, a time when old friends and distant family members came together again. People who had quarreled were expected to make up and become friends once again. However, Christian missionaries denounced

Many beliefs of the Plains Cree centered on the pipe stem bundle. Every band possessed at least one of these sacred objects.

the Sun Dance as a pagan ritual and had it outlawed. In 1884 an amendment of the Canadian Indian Act made the Sun Dance a criminal offense. It remained illegal until 1952.

The religion of the Cree now blends traditional rituals and beliefs with Christianity. Many Cree devoutly attend Christian church services, but others also attend and take part in Sun Dances and summer powwows. A large number of Cree practice traditional healing rituals along with modern medicine.

Here is a story about a small bird, which reflects the Cree view of nature and people:

The Robin

Many ages ago, there was only one fire in the world. It was kept burning by an old hunter who lived in a big forest. All the birds liked the fire because it was so warm. However, in that forest lived a bear who feared and hated the fire very much. The bear waited for his chance to get near enough to the fire to put it out. But he feared the old hunter's arrows and dared not approach when he was there.

One day the old man became very ill. He could not tend the fire. When the bear saw that the old man was helpless and the fire was getting low, he rushed forward and trampled the last of the flames. Once the fire was out, the bear lumbered away.

***H**aving converted to Christianity, many Cree now attend services at churches near their homes. Still, despite this influence, traditional beliefs endure.*

At the same time there was a little robin perched up in a tree. He saw what was happening, and he was very sad that the bear had destroyed the fire. He flew down to the ground and noticed that there was still a spark in the firepit. The bird flapped his wings, and the fire flared up once again.

As he rekindled the flames, however, the robin did not notice that his feathers had also caught fire. He flew away, and wherever he rested another fire started. So there came to be many fires throughout the land. And that is why the robin now has a red breast.

Games and Gambling

Cree children and adults enjoyed many athletic contests and games, which emphasized skill, intelligence, and strength. They played a kind of soccer on a field with two goals, each set about a hundred feet apart. Players tried to kick a head-sized ball made of buckskin and stuffed with animal hair across the opponent's goal. The main rule in this game was that no one was allowed to throw the ball. Some Cree people also played stickball, which was similar to modern-day lacrosse. In this game, they used rackets to fling a small ball into the opponent's goal.

Boys and men played many games related to hunting and warfare. In the otter hunting game, two men set up ten wooden figures of otters, each smaller than the other, and shot arrows at

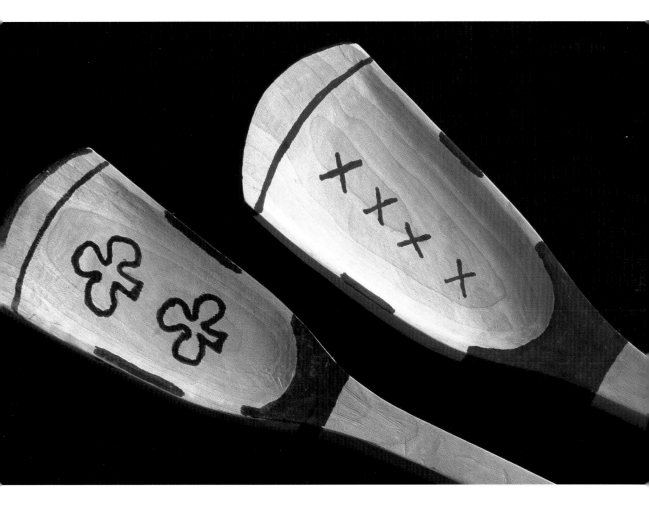

*T*he Cree enjoyed many toys as well as games involving balls and other objects. All of these items were handcrafted for the children often by their mothers and fathers.

them. The object of the game was to shoot the smallest otter. In the caribou hunting game, boys and men used sticks to flip pebbles at a board set up about six to ten feet away. About a foot long and six inches wide, the board represented a caribou. Sometimes, the Cree also used bows and arrows to shoot at this target.

In the goose hunting game, two boys sat in a blind, which was a place where hunters hid from approaching flocks of ducks and geese. Carrying goose feathers in their hands, two other boys approached from different directions. With flipping sticks, the two hunters then flung pebbles at the feathers. If one of his feathers was struck, the boy dropped it. Whoever hit the most feathers won this game. Related to this was the war game in which a man ran back and forth while the other warriors shot blunt arrows at him. Often played before going to war, this game helped boys and men to practice their shooting skills and their ability to dodge arrows.

Children amused themselves with many kinds of handcrafted toys, such as small bows, pea shooters, buzz toys, bull roarers, and carved wooden dolls. They played many games, such as hide and seek, tug of war, and the square game, which was similar to fox and geese. A square was made in the snow, and the person who was "it" stood in the center. The children called him "the cannibal." The other players stood in the corners. The object was to run from one corner to another without being touched by the cannibal. If the cannibal touched someone, that person then became "it."

Through the long winter, the Cree also played many games in

the warmth of their tipis. In *taphan*, which was similar to the cup and pin game, cone-shaped caribou bones were strung on a buckskin thong and tied to a bone or wooden striking pin. The object of the game was to toss the bones into the air and try to catch one of them on the striking pin. Bones tied farther away from the pin scored as many as ten points, while the closest bone scored only one point. People also liked to play hand games involving string figures, such as cat's cradle.

5. Changing World

The Cree way of life began to change dramatically as trappers and traders pushed deeper into the Cree ancestral homelands.

I could have been on the prairie yet if I had chosen. I am a man. Do as you like. I am in your power. I gave myself up. You did not catch me.

—Poundmaker at his trial in 1885

NOT LONG AFTER THE CREE CAME INTO CONTACT WITH BRITISH AND FRENCH traders, they began to suffer many tragedies, especially epidemics of European diseases against which they had little or no resistance. Because the various Cree bands were scattered over such a broad territory, the tribe managed to withstand these contagious diseases better than other native groups. However, many people still fell victim to these foreign illnesses. From 1780 to 1782, a smallpox epidemic raged through the Hudson Bay territory. Many people died in these epidemics, while the survivors were often attacked by enemies, including the Blackfeet, who raided Plains Cree camps weakened by so many sudden deaths.

When the Hudson's Bay Company and the North West Company merged in 1821, many Cree abandoned their nomadic way of life and settled near the trading posts. Over time, native communities grew up around the posts. In 1838 a second smallpox epidemic swept through the Cree bands, which were now living closer together. The Cree barely recovered from this epidemic before being struck with another wave of diseases ranging from tuberculosis to influenza. As many as a third of all Cree may have died in epidemics, which continued until the early twentieth century.

The Cree also had to deal with new religions, which challenged their ancestral beliefs. In the mid-1600s French Jesuit priests worked

Trade goods from the British and French improved daily life for the Cree, but the continued influence of outsiders eventually altered traditional customs and beliefs.

among the Swampy Cree for a time. However, the Cree were largely left alone until 1820, when both Protestant and Catholic missionaries began to accompany Hudson's Bay Company trading expeditions. These religious leaders encountered and converted many Cree. In 1823 the Church of England established its first churches in their territory. By the mid-nineteenth century, both Protestant and Catholic missionaries had become very active among the Cree, and eventually many members converted to Christianity. The missionaries actively tried to eliminate all native religions in favor of their own faith. They also devised a kind of alphabet called a syllabary that was widely accepted by the Cree. This syllabary helped to preserve the Cree language.

A number of Plains Cree bands resisted religious conversion and held onto their traditional beliefs and practices, such as the Sun Dance. Once the Plains Cree were confined to reserves, however, Christian missionaries worked with government officials to "civilize" them. The government passed laws that banned traditional beliefs, practices, and language. Officials also established a system of residential schools operated by missionaries. The practices of these schools were quite sinister. As Bishop Vital Grandin said of native children in 1875, "We instill in them a pronounced distaste for the native life so that they will be humiliated when reminded of their origin. When they graduate from our institutions, the children have lost everything Native except their blood."

In 1871 the Cree reluctantly signed the first of several treaties with the Canadian government. Over a span of fifty years, from 1871 to 1921, native people were forced to sign eleven treaties,

*L*iving on the open prairies, the Plains Cree struggled against the Canadian government to keep their territory and traditional ways of life.

which came to be known as the "Numbered Treaties." These treaties confined the Cree and other tribes to a certain territory and required them to remain peaceful. Many bands had to agree to settle on reserves established by the government, which allotted land based on the number of native people in each community. The government held this land in trust for each Cree group and administered tribal business through the Department of Indian Affairs. The government was supposed to supply rations to the tribes to prevent starvation, which had become widespread among many bands. The government also agreed to provide schools, agricultural equipment, and training, along with yearly payments called annuities.

In Treaty Number 6 of 1876, the Plains Cree finally submitted to the government's demands over the objections of their new chief, Poundmaker. In a speech during the treaty negotiations, Poundmaker stated, "The government mentions how much land is to be given to us. He says one square mile for each family, he will give us. This is our land! It isn't a piece of pemmican to be cut off and given in little pieces back to us. It is ours and we will take what we want." Three years later, however, Poundmaker accepted a small reserve west of Battleford, in present-day Saskatchewan.

For just over a century, buffalo had shaped the daily life of the Plains Cree. By the end of the nineteenth century, however, only a few small herds of buffalo remained. Epidemics also continued to ravage the Plains Cree as they settled on reserves and tried to farm the land. In 1880 Poundmaker mourned the great loss to his people: "We who are on the reserves now, when we do set to work, have so few cattle that one family goes to work, lots of others remain idle and we cannot put in much crop."

The Canadian government had agreed to provide livestock, seed grain, and agricultural implements, including plows and wagons. However, the Cree were given broken-down equipment and half-wild Montana cattle that could not be hitched to plows. Moreover, no mills were built in the region, where the Cree could store or market their wheat. Nonetheless, the Cree managed to increase their cattle herds and wheat farms until non-natives argued that the government was helping the Cree too much. In 1889 such extensive restrictions were placed on the Cree that many were forced to give up cattle ranching and wheat farming.

While the Plains Cree struggled with starvation, the other Cree bands continued to face their own challenges. Christian missionaries who arrived in Ontario in the late 1800s converted a large number of Woodland Cree, although many continued to practice their traditional beliefs. The missionaries and traders also brought more diseases.

Moreover, the number of beaver and caribou, which had supplied furs and food, plunged dramatically in Ontario. The government also enforced game laws that limited Cree hunting of geese and ducks. Unable to provide game for their families, many Cree families starved.

The Woodland Cree also had to contend with an increasing number of settlers in their ancestral territory, along with damage from mining and railroads. In August 1905, tribal leaders signed Treaty Number 9 at Moose Factory. This treaty applied to the Cree living in Ontario. Each person in the band was paid eight dollars upon signing and then given yearly payments of four dollars of "treaty money." In return, the Cree gave up all land rights, titles, and other privileges. However, the Cree apparently did not understand the language and terms of this treaty.

People began to move into clustered log cabins in which they established their own communities. They continued to elect their own chiefs—a practice that became mandatory in the 1920s. Although their sprawling lands were steadily whittled away, the Cree at least have managed to maintain many traditions, including hunting and fishing, to the present day.

Between 1920 and 1940 hundreds of Cree were still dying from tuberculosis, flu, measles, whooping cough, and other diseases. The Hudson's Bay Company did little to provide health care, even for its own employees. Although medicines and immunizations were provided to the Ontario Cree in the 1940s, health care and educational services remained inadequate.

To add to the problems, by the end of World War II the beaver and other fur-bearing animals in many of the lands of the Swampy Cree had been overtrapped. Many people had to move into nearby cities and towns such as Moosonee and Churchill. The lives of many Swampy Cree changed drastically as for the first time ever they attended school, received non-native medical care, accepted government aid, and came into contact with the world through new roads and airplanes. The construction of new roads and rail lines, along with the growing forestry industry, also increased pollution. The number of game animals plunged.

Northwest Rebellion

In 1884 Louis Riel became the Métis leader in the Canadian Northwest. A small group of Métis asked him to present their land claims to the Canadian government. When the government ignored the claims, Riel then tried to establish an independent nation of

*E*ven after the Cree came into contact with traders, they continued to live in tipis and travel in handmade birch-bark canoes.

Métis and native people in the Northwest. This action came to be known as the Northwest Rebellion of 1885, although Métis and native peoples called it the "Northwest Resistance."

The Canadian government did not provide Chief Big Bear and his starving band with adequate rations, supplies, and land for a reserve. So, although he had signed an earlier treaty, Big Bear joined Louis Riel and the Métis in their struggle for territory along the North and South Saskatchewan rivers. Having lost faith in the government, Big Bear's people built a warrior's lodge, which shifted leadership to Wandering Spirit—the war chief.

When the government failed to supply his band with rations and farming tools, Poundmaker also allowed his warriors to become involved in the Northwest Rebellion. On March 26, 1885, warriors in the tribes of Poundmaker and Big Bear joined the Métis in an uprising against the Canadian forces at Duck Lake. On April 2, 1885, Wandering Spirit led the Cree warriors into Frog Lake and requested food and supplies for his starving people from the Indian agent. When the agent refused to meet with the band, Wandering Spirit shot him. Hungry and frustrated, the warriors then ransacked the site, killing eight more settlers and a Métis in the Frog Lake Massacre.

A month later, Lieutenant Colonel William Otter led 350 Canadian troops against Poundmaker's camp in a surprise attack that came to be known as the Battle of Cut Knife Hill. Under the leadership of war chief Fine Day, a small group of warriors attacked the Canadians from several positions, which made Otter believe that he and his soldiers were outnumbered. Otter fled to Battleford,

When the Canadian government failed to provide food and supplies, the Plains Cree and Métis rose up in the Northwest Rebellion of 1885.

and Poundmaker convinced the warriors not to attack the retreating troops. He said to the warriors, "See all these women; see all these children; see all these young people who surround you. They are the ones that we must save. I know that you are brave. In fighting against the whites you can hinder them very much. But we will yield to the number, and something tells me that our children will have their lives safe."

In May 1885 government soldiers defeated the Métis in a four-day battle at Batoche, and two weeks later Louis Riel surrendered to face charges of treason. On August 1, 1885, a jury found him guilty. The jury recommended mercy, but Judge Hugh Richardson sentenced Riel to death. He was hanged in Regina, Saskatchewan, on November 16, 1885. On November 27, eight Cree warriors were hanged at Battleford after being convicted of murdering the settlers at Frog Lake.

On May 26, 1885, Poundmaker surrendered to Canadian authorities at Fort Battleford. Accused of treason, Poundmaker was tried in Regina. "I can't understand," he said at his trial, "how it is that after saving so many lives I am brought here." The fate of the great Cree chief symbolized the tragedy that befell native peoples on the Great Plains of Canada in the second half of the nineteenth century. After the two-day trial, he was found guilty and sentenced to prison for three years in Manitoba's Stoney Mountain Penitentiary. While Poundmaker was in prison, "Buffalo Bill" Cody wrote to Sir John A. Macdonald, Canada's first prime minister, asking for the Cree chief to be released so he could

Over time, Cree people abandoned traditional styles of clothing, moved into wood-frame homes, and adopted many other new ways.

become a star in his world-famous Wild West Show. Poundmaker was released due to illness in 1886 after serving less than a year. He died the same year.

After the Canadian soldiers put down the rebellion, Big Bear was also forced to surrender to government officials. He was tried in a Canadian court with a group of Cree warriors. At the trial he said, "I am old and ugly, but I have tried to do good. Pity the children of my tribe. Pity the old and helpless of my people. I speak with a single tongue; and because Big Bear has always been the friend of the white man, send out and pardon and give them help. I have spoken." However, eight of the Cree warriors, including Wandering Spirit, were hanged. Big Bear was found guilty of treason and sentenced to three years of hard labor. After serving half his sentence, he was released due to poor health. Suffering from sickness and despair, he died the following year.

After Big Bear surrendered, his son Imasees led the rest of the Big Bear band into Montana, where Imasees changed his name to Little Bear. In 1896 the U.S. government returned Little Bear and his "Canadian Indians" to Canada. However, a few weeks later, Little Bear and his band drifted back into Montana, where they joined a small Ojibwe band led by Rocky Boy. In 1916 the U.S. Congress authorized that a tract of abandoned military land be set aside as a reservation for the Little Bear/Rocky Boy band. The Rocky Boy reservation is located near the Canadian border, approximately thirty-one miles south of Havre, Montana. It was the smallest and last reservation established in Montana.

Cree Language

Cree is one of the most widely spoken native languages in North America. In the Algonquian family of languages, it is closely related to the languages of the Montagnais and the Naskapi and the languages spoken by many other tribes, including the Abenaki, Arapaho, Cheyenne, Delaware, Micmac, Potawatomi, and Shawnee.

If you go to a James Bay community such as Chisasibi, you will hear people speaking Cree, a language that is perhaps older than the pyramids of Egypt. And that language is still woven into the fabric of their culture. As Rodney A. Clifton wrote in *Semantic Structures in Cree Language*, "It can be argued that the native language spoken by an individual shapes the way in which he thinks about reality. The reality an individual observes is organized and becomes meaningful entirely in terms of the specific language he speaks."

J. Lor further explained in *Cree Traditions*, "Upon listening to our guides speak this ancient language, I could neither figure out whether or not it had an Asian or European sound. All I can say is that it was both musical and meaningful. I wished that I had more time to spend to learn how to say a few words."

Here are a few useful Cree words with their meanings in French and English, courtesy of the Chisasibi Mandow Agency in northern Quebec:

Cree	French	English
Chi sa si bi	Chisasibi	Chisasibi
Wat chia	bonjour	welcome
Wat chia	au revoir	good-bye
Chin is kum din	merci	thank you
Chi-sach-heetan	Je t'aime.	I love you.
idim ma bee suum	nord	north
besuum aw datche	sud	south
itch sdoo	ouest	west
waba noo datche	est	east
popoun	hiver	winter
sigoun	printemps	spring
niben	été	summer
degadjun	automne	fall

Cree	French	English
missitch stdoo nemass	grand poisson	big fish
ituk	caribou	caribou
nisk	oie	goose
min istuk	île	island
weena buk	Baie-James	James Bay
Chisasibi	Riviére Grande	Grande River
indohoo	chasse	hunt
inutch	aujourd'hui	today
wabatcha	demain	tomorrow
mistuk	arbre	tree
Tanasin casoine	Quel est ton nom?	What is your name?
Tan atoponazine	Quel âge as-tu?	How old are you?
Mio tchichigaw	C'est une belle journée.	It's a nice day.

6. New Ways

At the heart of the reserve near James Bay, the new tribal offices at Chisasibi reflect the traditional design of the Cree tipi.

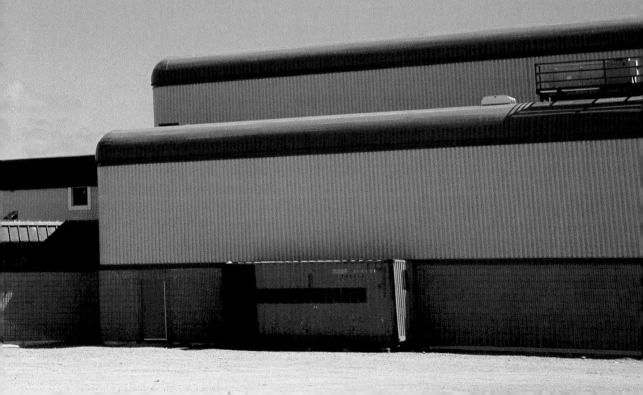

> We have so much to offer the rest of the world.
> —Elijah Harper, Cree leader

TODAY, THERE ARE ABOUT 200,000 CREE PEOPLE OFFICIALLY REGISTERED in Canada. Most live in Ontario and Quebec. However, these numbers do not include the 200,000 Canadian Métis. There are many "unofficial" bands or groups as well. About a third of Canada's native population and nearly 3 percent of the nation's general population is of Cree descent. Most of the Métis are of Cree origin and speak "Michif," a unique French-Cree creole that consists of French nouns and Cree verbs.

Many Cree individuals and bands have preserved their traditional beliefs and customs. Large groups, such as the Plains, Woodland, Swampy, and Moose Cree, continue to live in Canada. Today, there are Cree reserves in Quebec, Ontario, Manitoba, Alberta, and Saskatchewan. There are nine Cree villages in Quebec, each with its own chief. A grand chief oversees these nine villages and the Grand Council of the Cree of Quebec. There are also many bands throughout Canada, including the Calling River People, Rabbit Skin People, Cree-Assiniboine, Touchwood Hills People, House People, Parklands People, Upstream People, and Downstream People. There are more than sixty official Western Woods Cree bands with a total population of at least 35,000. In 1882 the Poundmaker Nation consisted of 164 members; today the membership stands at 1,115, with approximately 452 residing on the reserve. The Plains Cree also live on the Rocky Boy Chippewa-Cree Reservation in Chouteau and Hill counties in Montana.

Many Cree people work in offices on the reserve, while enjoying hunting, fishing, trapping, and other outdoor activities in their free time.

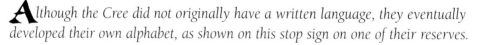

*A*lthough the Cree did not originally have a written language, they eventually developed their own alphabet, as shown on this stop sign on one of their reserves.

Hunting, fishing, and gathering are still vitally important to the Cree. Many people live at least part of the year in the bush, following the traditional seasonal rounds for these outdoor activities. The Cree are also involved in several industries, notably mining, transportation, logging, and commercial fishing. Some Plains Cree raise horses, while Cree bands in Quebec also operate a successful airline called Air Creebec. A number of Cree people work on the James Bay Hydroelectric Project in Quebec. Many other people are employed in government programs on reserves throughout Canada. Others supplement their income making fine handicrafts, such as carved wooden figures, bark baskets, and buckskin moccasins. However, because of their relative isolation and lack of industry, unemployment remains high in Cree communities. Reserve life continues to be harsh and demeaning. Many people live on welfare in government housing. They shop at a band store, send their children to a local school, and receive medical care at a nearby hospital, when necessary. With so few jobs available, many people have few opportunities on the reserve.

In recent years, Cree leaders have worked hard to achieve greater independence and control over their own services and resources. Many Cree now manage their own school system. About half of all Cree continue to speak their ancestral language, which is taught in these schools. However, people are still grappling with many critical issues, such as the destruction of natural resources on their lands, the need for economic development, and unsteady relationships with provincial and national governments. Clearcutting of forests has seriously damaged Cree hunting and trapping lands, disrupting their efforts to preserve their traditional way of life. The Cree are also dealing with chronic health problems and the need to improve medical care in many communities.

Cree bands continue to fight for their land rights. For example, the Lubicon Band never received the reserve and land rights promised to them in 1939. Their land around Lubicon Lake in northern Alberta abounds in oil, and in the 1970s, the band unsuccessfully fought to halt road construction to the drilling site. By the early 1980s hundreds of oil wells around their community were causing serious pollution.

*T*oday Cree children attend school on the reserves where they study traditional language and culture along with their other subjects.

Once a self-sufficient hunting community, the people must now depend on welfare. The band is seeking compensation for "irreparable damage to their way of life."

In 1971 the Quebec Cree protested the massive James Bay Hydroelectric Project, which called for damming the La Grande River and building several hydroelectric generating stations along the rapids. Electricity from this project would be transmitted south to Montreal and cities in the United States—over the objections of the Grand Council of the Crees. Fifty Cree and Inuit hunters opposed the project in Quebec courts, arguing that their way of life would be threatened. They won their case, but the ruling was overturned a week later and the project went ahead. In 1975 the Cree signed the James Bay and Northern Quebec Agreement, which required them to surrender 640,000 square kilometers of land in exchange for more than $230 million and special concessions, such as land ownership of more than 3,300 square kilometers, subsistence rights on more than 20,000 square miles, and a veto over mineral rights. When fully completed, the project, which many Cree still oppose, will affect a land area of more than 360,000 square kilometers.

Over the past thirty years, the Cree have been involved in similar clashes with the Canadian government—over culture, politics, and economics. A joint position paper written in 1975 by the Métis Society, Native Women, and Northern Municipal Council of Saskatchewan stated, "The Canadian government has created laws to maintain the system which oppresses us. The judicial system serves to legitimize these laws, and makes it appear that it is our

Many Cree families have homes in the reserve community as well as camps out in the countryside, where they live for part of the year.

fault that we are oppressed."

The Cree became the first people in the history of Canada to argue in court that the environment was integral to their way of life. Nearly 120 years after the 1885 conviction of Poundmaker, Cree leaders also have gone to the courts to seek a pardon for the chief. Tyrone Tootoosis, a member of the Poundmaker band and native leader with the First Nations Coalition for Accountability, is among those seeking the pardon. Tootoosis, who played the role of Poundmaker in a 1998 movie about Big Bear, argues that Poundmaker did not support the rebellion leader Louis Riel. In 1998 a bill was also introduced into the House of Commons to pardon the Métis leader Louis Riel, who was hanged for treason in 1885.

Through these ongoing efforts, the Cree have begun to help themselves and others better appreciate the land and heritage of native people. Their traditions have sustained them for thousands of years, and undoubtedly, through vigilance and hard work, will continue to do so long into the future.

More about

the Cree

In power boats instead of birch-bark canoes,
the Cree still make their way down rivers
and streams and along the edges of
many northern lakes.

Timeline

1611 Henry Hudson trades with the Cree while exploring James Bay.

about 1650 The Jesuits are the first Europeans to document contact with the Cree.

1670–1688 The Cree become active traders of European goods, after the Hudson's Bay Company is established near their territory.

1780–1782 Smallpox epidemic rages through the tribes in the Hudson Bay area.

1821 The North West Company merges with the Hudson Bay Company, which then monopolizes the fur trade.

1842 Poundmaker is born near Battleford, Saskatchewan.

1870 The Canadian government purchases land from the Hudson's Bay Company, and the homelands of the Cree and other native people becomes the Canadian frontier.

1871–1921 Cree reluctantly sign eleven "Numbered Treaties" with the Canadian government.

1876 Poundmaker becomes chief of a Cree band. Treaty Number 6 is signed in which the Plains Cree submit to many government demands in exchange for reserve lands, rations, services, and equipment.

1879 Poundmaker accepts a small reserve west of Battleford, in present-day west-central Saskatchewan.

1885 Louis Riel leads the Métis in an uprising against the Canadian government after Métis land claims are ignored. The Métis are defeated at Batoche, and Riel is found guilty of treason and hanged.

1886 Poundmaker dies on July 4, four months after being released from jail after serving less than a year of his sentence.

1899 Treaty Number 8 is signed by the Cree and Chipewyan peoples of Fort McMurray, exchanging hunting and trapping lands for reserves, tools, and payments.

1905 The province of Saskatchewan is formed by combining the North West Territory provisional districts of Assinboia, Saskatchewan, and Athabaska..

1958 The Federation of Saskatchewan Indians is formed by native groups in Saskatchewan.

1965 On May 13, Judge J. M. Policha rules that under the "Medicine Chest" provision of Treaty Number 6, the Canadian government must provide health care for all registered Indians in Saskatchewan living on and off reserves.

1971 The James Bay Hydroelectric Project is announced by Quebec premier Robert Bourassa. Cree and Inuit leaders protest in Quebec courts.

1974 A Quebec Supreme Court injunction briefly stops the massive James Bay Hydroelectric Project in northern Quebec from flooding large areas of Inuit and Cree territory. But when the ruling is overturned a week later, the project goes ahead as planned.

1996 Chief Poundmaker Historical Centre and Teepee Village is opened by Poundmaker Cree Nation on the reserve.

1998 On February 5, the Poundmaker Cree Nation is awarded a parcel of land by the Saskatchewan provincial government under the Saskatchewan Treaty Land Entitlement Framework Agreement.

2001 The 125th anniversary of the adoption of Treaty Number 6, which Poundmaker signed, is observed. A powwow is held at Duck Lake to mark the occasion.

Notable People

Big Bear (Mistihui'muskwa) (1825–1888), Plains Cree, chief of an Ojibwe and Cree band, was born near Fort Carleton at Jackfish, Saskatchewan. By the 1870s, when he was forty years old, he became chief of a band of mixed Ojibwe and Cree people. In 1876 the Canadian government sent a Methodist missionary named George McDougall to invite chiefs of the Cree bands to treaty negotiations. While Big Bear led the largest band, he was not invited, possibly because McDougall intentionally forgot chiefs such as Big Bear who refused to convert to Christianity. Big Bear still went to the negotiations, but when he arrived the other chiefs had already signed the treaty with the Canadian government. Big Bear at first opposed Treaty Number 6 and left without signing his name. At a council of two thousand natives peoples at Poundmaker's reserve in Cut Knife, he denounced the Canadian government and urged a united stand by his followers.

However, when his people faced starvation, Big Bear later conceded and signed the treaty. Yet, by 1885, conditions had still not improved for Big Bear and his people, largely because the Canadian government failed to provide the band with adequate rations and land for a reserve. Big Bear then became one of the few native people in western Canada to lead an uprising. His band joined Louis Riel's Métis in their 1885 struggle for territory along the North and South Saskatchewan rivers.

Big Bear was forced to surrender when the Canadian government put down the rebellion. He was tried in a Canadian court and found guilty of treason. He was sentenced to three years of hard labor. After serving half his sentence, he was released due to poor health. Suffering from sickness and despair, he died the following year.

Matthew Coon Come (1956–), Cree leader, was born as a dog sled carrying his mother raced to a camp on his father's trap line. At age six, he was sent away to a boarding school. When he was sixteen, he read about threats to the ancestral land of his birth and became active in fighting for

Big Bear

native rights in Canada. He fought against the massive $13 billion hydroelectric project in northern Quebec. He read that one of the reservoirs was going to be built in his community and said, "Our home is going to be under water." He later graduated from Trent University in Ontario and studied law at McGill University before returning to his community to become deputy chief of the James Bay Cree People. He subsequently became chief of the group and has been reelected four times. In 1987 he was also first elected as grand chief of the Grand Council of the Crees and chairman of the Cree Regional Authority. In 1994 he received the Goldman Prize, which is considered the Nobel Prize of environmental awards. In 1995 he received the National Aboriginal Achievement Award, and in 1998 Trent University honored Coon Come with a Doctor of Laws Honoris Causa in recognition of his work. In 2000 he became the leader of all native people in Canada when he was elected national chief of the Assembly of First Nations.

He and his wife, Maryann Matoush, whom he married in 1976, have three daughters and two sons. Both he and his wife were taught by their parents how to live in the wilderness. Until they moved to Ottawa, they thrived on their territory in moosehide coats and snowshoes. Over the course of his life, Matthew Coon Come has perhaps been most noted for his international work in protecting the traditional ways of life of native people. He is now actively involved in convincing the Canadian government to honor its two hundred years of treaties in providing more land and independence to the Cree and other native peoples.

Fine Day (1850–193?), Plains Cree, war chief, was born of Cree parents in the Battle River area in Saskatchewan. As he grew up, he became a highly skilled warrior, shaman, and eventually war chief of the Poundmaker Cree band. During the Northwest Resistance in 1885, some of Poundmaker's followers raided the town of Battleford, Saskatchewan. Fearing retaliation from the Canadians, the warriors built a war lodge and sought Fine Day as their leader. Fine Day moved the band's camp to

Cut Knife Hill. At dawn on May 2, Lieutenant Colonel Otter led 350 Canadian soldiers in an attack on the Cree camp. Fine Day and his warriors charged the Canadians from several directions. Otter thought they must have five hundred warriors, but there were only fifty. Otter ordered a quick retreat of the Canadian Army at Cut Knife Hill. When native resistance ended, Fine Day went to live with the Sweetgrass Cree Band near Battleford and eventually became their chief. In 1934, when Fine Day was eighty-four, American anthropologist David Mandelbaum documented his recollections, some of which were published in a 1973 booklet entitled *My Cree People*. Fine Day's memoirs are a valuable firsthand account of Plains Cree life.

Fine Day

Piapot (Payepot, "One Who Knows the Secrets of the Sioux") (1816–1908), Plains Cree, war chief, medicine man, and resistance leader, was raised by his grandmother after his parents died of smallpox. He and his grandmother were captured by the Sioux and lived with them for fourteen years until freed by a Cree war party. Because of his knowledge of Sioux customs and territory, Piapot became an important war chief in raids against Sioux bands.

In 1870 Piapot and his seven hundred warriors were soundly defeated by the Blackfeet. In 1875 he reluctantly signed Treaty Number 4, which ceded Cree territory in the Qu'appell Valley of Manitoba. Piapot then moved his band farther west to what is now Saskatchewan. In 1882 in an act of defiance, Piapot's warriors yanked up survey stakes along a thirty-mile stretch of the Canadian Pacific Railway west of Moose Jaw. The following year, Piapot had his band set up their tipis in the path of the crew that was laying track. The Mounties drove the Piapot and his people away, then knocked down their tipis. Piapot and his band eventually settled near Regina. Although he strongly resented the settling of Cree territory, Piapot kept his warriors out of the Second Riel Rebellion of 1885 unlike Big Bear and Poundmaker. Government officials removed Piapot as band leader after his people held a Sun Dance, which was forbidden under Canadian law. However, his people continued to regard him as their leader. He was also honored by Manitoba officials in 1901.

Piapot

Poundmaker (Pitikwahanapiwiyin)

(1842–1886), Plains Cree, head chief, leader in the Riel Rebellion of 1885, was born near Battleford, Saskatchewan, to a shaman father and a Métis mother. He was named for his special talent for making pounds, which were pens for trapping buffalo. When Poundmaker was about thirty years old, Crowfoot, chief of the Blackfeet, adopted him to replace one of his sons who had been killed in battle. A gifted orator and diplomat, Poundmaker counseled peaceful relations with settlers moving into Cree territory. In 1876 he convinced the Canadian government to add a "famine clause" to Treaty Number 6. Although Poundmaker still mistrusted the government, he finally signed the treaty at the urging of his followers. He settled with his people on a reserve near his birthplace, but when the government failed to supply his band with rations and farming tools, Poundmaker became fed up with government policies. In 1885 he allowed members of his band to become involved in resistance activities. Under the leadership of Fine Day, the band drove back a surprise attack by the Canadian Army at Cut Knife Hill. Fine Day then wanted to join the Métis in their resistance against the government, and he tried to lead the Plains Cree band to the Métis camp at Batoche. However, Poundmaker delayed the band until the Métis had been defeated, and he then surrendered to Canadian authorities. Accused of treason, he was tried in Regina, Saskatchewan, and after two days the court found Poundmaker guilty. The judge sentenced him to three years' imprisonment in Manitoba's Stoney Mountain Penitentiary. He was released after less than a year due to poor health. Upon his release, he married Stony Woman, a woman

Poundmaker

much younger than he. Poundmaker and Stony Woman then walked most of the 250 miles to visit Crowfoot, his adoptive father and friend because they had just one horse between them. Poundmaker died just four months after the time of his release.

Louis Riel (1844–1885), French-Canadian Métis leader, was born in present-day Manitoba. He studied law and for the priesthood, but never finished his training in either profession. In 1875 he was exiled from Canada because of his role in the execution of a Canadian named Thomas Scott. Riel traveled to Indianapolis and Washington, D.C., where he sought support from the U.S. government. When he returned to Quebec, he entered an asylum and began to refer to himself as "The Prophet of the New World." Riel believed that he had a calling to lead the Métis people of the Canadian northwest. Although only one-eighth native, Riel became an ardent supporter of native rights, especially Métis rights. In 1884 a small group of Métis asked him to present their grievances regarding land claims to the Canadian government. However, the government ignored these concerns until

Louis Riel

Riel established a provisional government, which quickly escalated tensions between the Métis and the federal authorities. In May 1885, government soldiers defeated the Métis in a four-day battle at Batoche, and two weeks later Riel surrendered to face charges of treason. On August 1, 1885, a jury found him guilty, but recommended mercy. Nonetheless, Judge Hugh Richardson sentenced Riel to death. The court dismissed appeals, and a reexamination of Riel's mental state found him sane. He was hanged in Regina on November 16, 1885. His execution was widely opposed in Quebec, where sympathy for the French-speaking Canadian was strong. A prolific writer of poetry and letters, Riel kept journals most of his life, many of which have been published. Every summer, the city of Saskatoon, Saskatchewan, holds an annual sports and cultural celebration called Louis Riel Day.

Buffy Sainte-Marie (1942?–), folksinger and songwriter, was born in either 1941 or 1942 in Craven, Saskat chewan. She was orphaned as an infant and raised by a Micmac couple in Mass-achusetts. She studied Eastern philosophy in college, but had long wanted to become a singer and musician. She began playing the guitar and writing songs when she was sixteen. Inspired by the warm reception to her work, she moved to New York and began singing in many folk clubs in Greenwich Village. She was soon offered a recording contract with Vanguard Records. Over the

Buffy Sainte-Marie

years, she had many hit songs, such as "Universal Soldier" and "Until It's Time for You to Go." Her 1992 recording, entitled *Confidence and Likely Stories*, emphasizes string music and complex rhythms that are markedly different from her earlier folk songs. Much of her work is concerned with native issues and rights. She has contributed writings to numerous Native American publications, and she is the author of *Nokosis and the Magic Hat* (1986), a children's book set on a reservation. Buffy lives in Hilo, Hawaii.

Wandering Spirit (Kapapamahchakwew) (1845–1885), Plains Cree, war chief of the Big Bear Band, was born near Jackfish Lake, Saskatchewan. When he was still a young man, Wandering Spirit distinguished himself as a warrior. During his life, he killed fifteen Blackfeet warriors, who were the Cree's traditional enemy. After he became war chief of the Big Bear Nation in the late 1870s, Wandering Spirit remained hostile toward settlers, especially for their role in killing off the buffalo. In 1880, on a hunting expedition in Montana, he met Louis Riel, who tried to convince Wandering Spirit that the Cree and the Métis should become allies in driving settlers from the Great Plains and establishing their own independent nation. In 1885 Wandering Spirit again voiced his anger with Thomas Quinn, the Indian agent at Frog Lake, Saskatchewan. Quinn had a strict "no work, no food" policy toward the Cree. On April 2, Wandering Spirit led his warriors into

Wandering Spirit

policy toward the Cree. On April 2, Wandering Spirit led his warriors into Frog Lake, where he shot Quinn, and his followers then killed eight non-natives and one Métis. Wandering Spirit surrendered at Fort Pitt in early July and was tried for murder. He had no lawyer to defend him, and he admitted killing Quinn but refused to offer any explanation. On September 24, 1885, Judge Charles Rouleau stated, "The sentence of the court is that you, Wandering Spirit, be taken back to jail till Friday the 27th day of November, and then be taken to the scaffold and there be hanged by the neck until you are dead; and may God have mercy on your soul." The day before his execution, Wandering Spirit told a journalist that he did not fear death, but did not want to enter the afterlife with a ball and chain on his ankle. He was greatly relieved to learn that it would be removed before he was hanged. Wandering Spirit was hanged November 27, 1885, at Battleford, Saskatchewan. According to Cree tradition, Wandering Spirit did not sing his death song as he stood on the scaffold, but a love song for his wife.

Glossary

ahtchak   A person's soul.

Algonquian   Group, or "family," of more than twenty languages that is one of the most widespread and commonly spoken throughout North America. Many Native American tribes speak Algonquian languages, including the Cree.

Atayohkanak   Lesser spirits of animals and plants that served as intermediaries between people and the Creator, Kitchi-Kitchi-Manito.

babiche   Cord made from rawhide used in making shoes.

breechcloth   A rectangular piece of buckskin worn by men; also called breechclout.

buffalo pound   A fenced, circular trap usually made of brush and hides, with a funnel-shaped fence leading up to its entrance.

fur trade   Network through which the Cree and other native people exchanged animal furs, notably beaver pelts, with the British and French.

Great Plains   A vast area of prairie stretching across the central part of North America from Texas to Canada.

Jesuit   A priest in the Society of Jesus, a Roman Catholic order founded by Saint Ignatius Loyola in 1534.

Kitchi-Kitchi-Manito   Great-Great Spirit, the Cree creator.

lacrosse   Modern sport based on a stickball game, which was popular among Native American tribes living in eastern North America.

Matchi-Manito   Evil Spirit, resembling the devil, to whom the Cree made sacrifices.

Métis   A person of mixed Euro-American (usually French or English) and American Indian (often Cree) ancestry, especially in western Canada.

michwaup   A summer tipi made with cedar or spruce poles and a canvas covering.

moccasins   Soft leather shoes often decorated with brightly colored quillwork or beads.

muhtukan   A rectangular winter home made of logs and sod.

muskeg   Northern boggy land, typically with spruce trees and sphagnum moss.

Numbered Treaties   Series of treaties between native peoples across Canada and the government.

powwow   A modern Native American gathering featuring dancers and drum groups.

reserves   Parcels of land set aside for native peoples and held in trust by the Canadian government. Called reservations in the United States.

shaman   A holy person responsible for the spiritual and physical healing of tribal members. Also called healer or medicine man.

Sun Dance   A sacred ceremony held every summer in which the Plains Cree gave thanks for their good fortune.

sweat lodge   A dome-shaped hut covered with animal skins in which individuals purified themselves.

taphan   A winter game played indoors with caribou bones and a bone or wooden striking pin.

tipi   A cone-shaped home made of poles covered with animal skins.

travois   A sledlike carrier made from two long poles tied together to make an A-shaped frame pulled by dogs and later horses to transport tipis and belongings from one place to another.

vision quest   A ritual in which individuals went off alone to fast and pray with hopes of having a vision in which their spirit helper is revealed to them.

wigwam   A domed house made of a wooden frame covered with bark or animal skins.

Wisahketchak   Trickster Spirit, who could bring good luck or misfortune to people.

Further Information

Readings

The following books and Web sites were consulted in the research and writing of *The Cree*. The story entitled "The Creation" was adapted from a story originally collected by Fred Swindlehurst and published in the *Journal of American Folklore,* v. 18, 1905. "The Robin" was adapted by a story collected by J. R. Cresswell and published in the *Journal of American Folklore,* v. 36, 1923.

Ahenakew, Alice, Freda Ahenakew, and H. Christoph Wolfar. *Âh-âyîtaw isi ê-kî-kiskêyihtahkik maskihkiy (They Knew Both Sides of Medicine: Cree Tales of Curing and Cursing.)* Winnipeg: University of Manitoba Press, 2000.

Beardy, Flora, and Robert Coutts. *Voices from Hudson Bay: Cree Stories from York Factory.* Montreal; Buffalo, NY: McGill-Queen's University Press, 1996.

Bloomfield, Leonard. *Sacred Stories of the Sweet Grass Cree.* New York: AMS Press, 1976, 1930.

Brass, Eleanor, and Henry Nanooch. *Medicine Boy and Other Cree Tales.* Calgary: Glenbow Museum, 1978.

Brightman, Robert Alain. *Grateful Prey: Rock Cree Human-Animal Relationships.* Berkeley: University of California Press, 1993.

Burford-Mason, Roger. *Travels in the Shining Island: The Story of James Evans and the Invention of the Cree Syllabary Alphabet.* Toronto: Natural Heritage Books, 1996.

Campbell, Maria. *Halfbreed.* Lincoln: University of Nebraska Press, 1982.

Cardinal, Phyllis. *The Cree People.* Edmonton: Duval House, 1998.

Darnell, Regna. "Plains Cree," in *Handbook of North American Indians.* Volume

13 (Plains, ed. Raymond J. Demallie) part 1, pp. 638–51. Washington, D.C.: Smithsonian Institution, 2001.

Dempsey, Hugh Aylmer. *Big Bear: The End of Freedom*. Lincoln; Vancouver, British Columbia: University of Nebraska Press; Douglas & McIntyre, 1984.

Dusenberry, Verne. *The Montana Cree: A Study in Religious Persistence*. Norman: University of Oklahoma Press, 1998, 1962.

Encyclopedia of North American Indians. Tarrytown, NY: Marshall Cavendish, 1997.

Flannery, Regina. *Ellen Smallboy: Glimpses of a Cree Woman's Life*. Montreal; Buffalo, NY: McGill-Queen's University Press, 1995.

Georgekish, Fred. *Iiyiyuu Miichiwaahp-h (Traditional Architecture of the Wemindji Cree)*. Wemindji, Quebec: Cree Nation of Wemindji, 1996.

Helm, June, ed. *Handbook of North American Indians*. Volume 6 (Subarctic). Washington, D.C: Smithsonian Institution, 1981. (See articles "East Main Cree," "West Main Cree," and "Western Woods Cree.")

Johansen, Bruce E., and Donald A. Grinde, Jr. *The Encyclopedia of Native American Biography*. New York: Henry Holt and Co., 1997.

Linderman, Frank Bird. *Indian Old-Man Stories: More Sparks from War Eagle's Lodge-Fire*. Lincoln: University of Nebraska Press, 2001, 1920.

Lytwyn, Victor P. *Muskekowuck Athinuwick: Original People of the Great Swampy Land*. Winnipeg: University of Manitoba Press, 2002.

Malinowski, Sharon, and Anna Sheets. *The Gale Encyclopedia of Native American Tribes*. Detroit, MI: Gale Research, 1998.

Malinowski, Sharon. *Notable Native Americans*. Detroit, MI: Gale Research, 1995.

McDonald, Frederick R. *Ancestral Portraits: The Colour of My People*. Calgary: University of Calgary Press, 2002.

Milloy, John Sheridan. *The Plains Cree: Trade, Diplomacy, and War, 1790 to 1870*. Winnipeg: University of Manitoba Press, 1990, 1988.

Morantz, Toby Elaine. *An Ethnohistoric Study of Eastern James Bay Cree Social Organization, 1700–1850*. Ottawa: National Museums of Canada, 1983.

———. *The White Man's Gonna Getcha: The Colonial Challenge to the Crees in Quebec*. Montreal: McGill-Queen's University Press, 2002.

Niezen, Ronald. *Defending the Land: Sovereignty and Forest Life in James Bay Cree Society*. Boston: Allyn and Bacon, 1998.

Pettipas, Katherine. *Severing the Ties That Bind: Government Repression of Indigenous Religious Ceremonies on the Prairies*. Winnipeg: University of Manitoba Press, 1994.

Pritzker, Barry M. *Native Americans: An Encyclopedia of History, Culture, and Peoples*. Santa Barbara, CA: ABC-CLIO, 1998.

Richardson, Boyce. *Strangers Devour the Land: A Chronicle of the Assault Upon the Last Coherent Hunting Culture in North America, the Cree Indians of Northern Quebec, and Their Vast Primeval Homelands*. New York: Knopf, 1976.

Russell, Dale R. *Eighteenth Century Western Cree and Their Neighbours*. Hull, Quebec: Canadian Museum of Civilization, 1991.

Sam-Cromarty, Margaret. *Légendes et Poèmes Indiens (Indian Legends and Poems)*. Val-d'Or, Quebec: D'ici et D'ailleurs, 1996.

Scott, Simeon, and C. D. Ellis. *Âtalôhkâna Nêsta Tipâcimôwina (Cree Legends and Narratives): From the West Coast of James Bay*. Winnipeg: University of Manitoba Press, 1995.

Tarasoff, Koozma J. *Persistent Ceremonialism: The Plains Cree and Saulteaux*. Ottawa: National Museums of Canada, 1980.

Taylor, J. Garth. *Canoe Construction in a Cree Cultural Tradition*. Ottawa: National Museums of Canada, 1980.

Van Stone, James W. *The Simms Collection of Plains Cree Material Culture from Southeastern Saskatchewan*. Chicago: Field Museum of Natural History, 1983.

Waldman, Carl. *Who Was Who in Native American History: Indians and Non-Indians from Early Contacts through 1900*. New York: Facts on File, 1990.

Wiebe, Rudy Henry. *Stolen Life: The Journey of a Cree Woman*. Toronto: Knopf Canada, 1998.

Children's Books

Ballantyne, Bill. *Wesakejack and the Flood*. Winnipeg: Bain & Cox, Publishers, 1994.

Brass, Eleanor. *Medicine Boy and Other Cree Tales*. Calgary: Glenbow-Alberta Institute, 1979.

Hodgins, Ken. *The Art of the Nehiyawak: Exploring the Art and Crafts of the Woods Cree*. Edmonton: Plains Publishing, 1988.

Karp, Barry. *People of the Muskeg: The Cree of James Bay*. Toronto: Nelson Canada, 1985.

Littlechild, George. *This Land Is My Land*. Emeryville, CA: Children's Book Press, 1993.

Loyie, Oskiniko Larry. *As Long as the River Flows: A Last Summer before Residential School*. Toronto: Groundwood Books, 2002.

Newton, Joanne Willis. *Aatiyuuhkaan: Legends of the Eastern James Bay Cree*. Chisasibi, Quebec: James Bay Cree Cultural Education Centre, 1989.

Norman, Howard A. *Trickster and the Fainting Birds*. San Diego, CA: Harcourt Brace, 1999.

————. *Who-Paddled-Backward-With-Trout*. Boston: Joy Street Books, 1987.

Oliviero, Jamie. *The Fish Skin*. New York: Hyperion Books for Children, 1993.

Owens, Della. *Going to Visit Kou-Kum*. Moberly Lake, British Columbia: Twin Sisters Publishing, 1994.

Pachano, Jane. *Changing Times*. Chisasibi, Quebec: James Bay Cree Cultural Education Centre, 1985.

————. *Chikabash*. James Bay, Quebec: James Bay Cree Cultural Education Centre, 1987.

————. *Waupsh*. Chisasibi, Quebec: James Bay Cree Cultural Education Centre, 1984.

Riehecky, Janet. *The Cree Tribe*. Mankato, MN: Bridgestone Books, 2003.

Robinson, Deborah B. *The Cree of North America*. Minneapolis, MN: Lerner Publications, 2001.

Ryan, Marla Felkins. *Cree*. San Diego, CA: Blackbirch Press, 2003.

Siy, Alexandra. *The Eeyou: People of Eastern James Bay*. New York: Dillon Press, 1993.

Willis-Newton, Joanne. *Now and Then*. James Bay, Quebec: James Bay Cree Cultural Education Centre, 1987.

Wood, Douglas. *Rabbit and the Moon*. New York: Simon & Schuster Books for Young Readers, 1998.

Organizations

Chisasibi Mandow Agency
P.O. Box 720
Chisasibi, Quebec J0M 1E0
Phone: (819) 855-3373
Fax: (819) 855-3374

Cree Nation of Eastmain
P.O. Box 90147
Shabow Meskino
Eastmain, Quebec J0M 1W0
Phone: (819) 977-0211/0266
Fax: (819) 977-0281

Cree Nation of Mistissini
Isaac Shecapio Sr. Administration Building
187 Main Street, Mistissini, Quebec G0W 1C0
Phone: (418) 923-3253
Fax: (418) 923-3115

Cree Nation of Wemindji
16 Beaver Road
Wemindji, Quebec J0M 1L0
Phone: (819) 978-0264
Fax: (819) 978-0265

Lucky Man Cree Nation
103-103B Packham Avenue
Saskatoon, SK S7N 4K4
Phone: (306) 374-2828
Fax: (306) 934-2853

Mikisew Cree First Nation
Box 90
Ft. Chipewyan, Alberta T0P 1B0
Phone: (780) 697-3740
Fax: (780) 697-3826

Norway House Cree Nation
P.O. Box 250
Norway House, Manitoba R0B 1B0
Phone: (204) 359-6786
Fax: (204) 359-4186

Oujè-Bougoumou
203 Opemiska Meskino
P.O. Box 131
Oujè-Bougoumou, Quebec G0W 3C0
Phone: (418) 745-3905
Fax: (418) 745-3544

Rocky Boy's Reservation
Chippewa-Cree Tribe
P. O. Box 544
Box Elder, MT 59521
Phone: (406) 395-4282
Fax: (406) 395-4497

Tataskweyak Cree Nation
General Delivery
Split Lake, Manitoba R0B 1P0
Phone: (204) 342-2045
Fax: (204) 342-2270

Waswanipi Communications
Waswanipi, Quebec J0Y 3C0
Phone: (819) 753-2557
Fax: (819) 753-2555

Woodland Cree First Nation
General Delivery
Cadotte Lake, Alberta T0H 0N0
Phone: (780) 629-3803
Fax: (780) 629-3898

York Factory First Nation
York Landing, Manitoba R0B 2B0
Phone: (204) 341-2180
Fax: (204) 341-2322

Web Sites

Chapleau Cree First Nation
http://www.geocities.com/chapleaucree/

Chippewa Cree Tribal Council
http://tlc.wtp.net/chippewa.htm

Chisasibi Mandow Agency
http://www.mandow.ca/

Cree Cultural Institute
http://www.creeculture.ca/e/institute/index.html

Cree Nation of Mistissini
http://www.nation.mistissini.qc.ca/

Cree Nation of Oujè-Bougoumou
http://www.ouje.ca/expo2000/index.html

Cree Nation of Wemindji
http://www.wemindji-nation.qc.ca/

CreeIndian.com
http://www.creeindian.com/

The Grand Council of the Crees
http://www.gcc.ca/

Lucky Man Cree Nation
http://www.luckyman.ca/

Mikisew Cree First Nation
http://www.mikisew.ca/

Nehinawe Speak Cree
http://www.nisto.com/cree/

Oujè-Bougoumou
http://www.ouje.ca/expo2000/index.html

The Plains Cree
http://www.schoolnet.ca/aboriginal/Plains_Cree/index-e.html

Woodland Cree First Nation
http://www.woodlandcree.com/index.htm

York Factory First Nation
http://york_factory_fn_304.tripod.com/YorkFactoryFN.html

Index

Page numbers in **boldface** are illustrations.